Canada and Noord-Brabant:
an eternal bond

Dr Jan A.F.M. Luijten

Canada and Noord-Brabant: an eternal bond

2002 Uitgeverij Aspekt

Cover background image:
The Wouwsche Plantage and the HQ in Bergen op Zoom.
Insert: Sergeant A.E. Halkyard M.M., 'Halkey', the Canadian on the Stuart the author saw on 27 October 1944 at 03.15 in the afternoon.

Canada and Noord-Brabant: an eternal bond
© 2002 Dr Jan A.F.M. Luijten
© 2002 Uitgeverij Aspekt bv
Amersfoortsestraat 27, 3769 AD Soesterberg
aspekt@knoware.nl
www.uitgeverijaspekt.nl
Cover design: Peter Koch
Inside: Van Swieten & Partner, Nieuwegein
ISBN: 90-5911-061-7

All rights reserved. No part of this publication may be reproduced in any form or by any means without the written permission of the publisher.

INDEX

7   The Battle of the Lost Patrol

33 The Rosary Para from Germany:
    how Bergen op Zoom was spared

53 Kapelsche Veer: where Seeking after Prestige can lead to

71 Literature

73 Appendix

This booklet could not have been written without the assistance and advice of a number of people, to whom my sincere gratitude is acknowledged for helping me to prepare and complete it.

The Battle
of the Lost Patrol

Bergen op Zoom, 1944

Friday, October 27, 1944, a beautiful sunny autumn day, a quarter past three in the afternoon; I was a 12 year old boy, standing at the front door of our house, Bolwerk Zuid 50, Bergen op Zoom, when I suddenly saw a Canadian Stuart Reconnaisance Tank at the opposite side of the street. That was the very moment I realised that we were liberated.

How that armoured vehicle got there was not clear to me. Two Canadian soldiers jumped out of the tank. A couple of neighbours came out to greet them, the Canadians probably wanted to know if there were still Germans about. I saw them shaking hands with the Canadians, who then got straight back into their tank. The vehicle turned on its axis and disappeared.

That same day Canadian Forces took over the streets and parks, but were stopped by the River de Zoom, which ran about 200 meters north of our house. The *Sprengcommando* had dynamited the bridges early in the morning.

The people of Bergen op Zoom had been living in cellars since the middle of October as the town was within the advance firing range of the approaching Canadian troops. Several houses had been hit and partially destroyed. Our house was saved, but a garden wall in our backyard was destroyed by a shell. If that shell had gone 10 centimeters

Sgt. Charles D. Kipp. Lincoln and Welland Regiment, 4th Canadian Armoured Division, Maldegem, Belgium, September 1944. PHOTO COURTESY: MARGARET KIPP

higher, it would have cleared the wall and landed on our cellar, in which case I would probably not have survived the war.

The Canadians had been blocked in their advance about 10 kilometers south of Bergen op Zoom by German forces defending the Kreekrakdam, the dam linking the province of Brabant to Beveland. For the Germans it was of the utmost importance to keep Beveland and Walcheren, in order to block the approach to the harbour of Antwerp. During this period the Canadians suffered heavy losses in a tank battle in the Wouwse Plantage, near the dam.

On Saturday, October 28, our cellar became a communication and information centre for the Canadians and the Dutch Underground Forces, because my father – a teacher of English – was one of the few local people who could serve as interpreter. He used his maps of the area to show where the Canadians could penetrate the German defences and cross the river. One of the Canadians who took part in the deliberations was Sergeant Charles Kipp of the Lincoln and Welland Regiment.

His commanding officer was Captain Lambert, an American serving in the Canadian army. I remember him sitting on the steps of our cellar as they discussed further action. There was the sound of shelling from outside, and the smell of gunpowder drifting into the cellar. One plan that they discussed was to use a crossing point close to a potash factory west of our house, as we knew there was a small dam in the River de Zoom, which had perhaps been overlooked by the *Sprengcommando*. A member of the underground forces, a man from Halsteren north of the river, who somehow had managed to get across the River de Zoom, warned us that this crossing point was heavily defended by young fanatics of the Hermann Goering Brigade.

After about a quarter of an hour, Lambert left to discuss this crossing point with his commander, Lieutenant Colonel Cromb.

After that Sgt. Kipp and a young corporal began to prepare for battle.

My father poured three glasses of claret as a toast to their success in battle. His hand was the only one that trembled as they raised their glasses. When he asked them why their hands were so steady, although they were facing possible death, they answered in perfect unison: 'Because we are Canadians,' indicating their pride in the fighting qualities of Canadians compared even to their non-Canadian allies.

That expression of patriotism became the title of the book which Charles wrote about his war time experiences several decades later.

Soon after that toast Kipp and his corporal disappeared into the twilight. Charles' book was dedicated to that nameless corporal who never returned from the battle.

We didn't see Kipp again till late on Sunday afternoon when he came back to our house, completely exhausted, and slept for almost two days in our sitting room.

So it was Tuesday before he said goodbye and left us to rejoin his unit. Before he left he told us that the hand- to-hand combat in the factory had been heavier than the fighting at the Falaise-gap in Normandy.

What exactly had happened and where became clear to us only many years later.

The Canadians had managed to cross the river on the Monday , and for some weeks Bergen op Zoom was under shellfire from the retreating German forces. Bergen op Zoom was in the approach route of buzzbombs destined for Antwerp from the beginning of November 1944 until the middle of March 1945. Two of these flying bombs landed in the city and destroyed two blocks of houses, killing dozens of people.

In the years that followed we sometimes wondered whether Charles had survived the Second World War. The means of communication after the war, however, were poor, so we never thought of making a search for him.

In 1984 Canadian war veterans visited Bergen op Zoom. They, as well as the inhabitants of the town, had changed in the intervening 40 years, so that it was difficult to recognise each other. It was only when you still remembered a name that you could trace a Canadian soldier, and luckily, that was the case with my father. And so he was able to find Charles Kipp. It was an emotional reunion between the soldier and the almost ninety year old Dutchman with whom Charles had drunk a toast forty years earlier.

In 1986 Kipp came back again . It was only then that we discovered where the battle had been fought, namely not in the potash factory as we had thought , but in a stove factory and an adjoining gin factory several miles to the east of our house.

The story that follows is the result of conversations with Kipp in 1986 and of talks with him three months before his

HQ of Colonel Gordon Dorward de Salaberry Wotherspoon, 'Swatty', and Lieutenant-Colonel William 'Bill' Cromb. In front of the hotel a Sherman tank.

PHOTO COURTESY: L.P. ROOSENBOOM

death in January 2000. The writer visited Charles Kipp – then 80 years old – in October 1999 in his house in Brownsville, Ontario, Canada. With the help of Lynda Sykes, Kipp had written a book about his experiences during the Second World War , which he completed in the summer of 1999.

Many of the details of the battle described hereafter are derived from this book and from correspondence between Kipp and the German Lieutenant Holst.

A battle of madmen in the dark

After leaving our house Kipp collected the men of his unit, A Company, which numbered about 30 men. Under the command of Lambert they went to the east and thus not to the potash factory. Kipp therefore immediately asked Lambert: 'Aren't we going in the wrong direction?' to which Lambert answered: 'No, the plan has been changed.'

The Company reached the outer edge of the town and halted at the eastern side of the railway line to Roosendaal. This stretch of railway runs along the top of a dyke. The River de Zoom is on the eastern side of the dyke. The men stopped where the narrow river curves to the west underneath the railway, whose rails here form a kind of bridge over the water, a bridge overlooked by the *Sprengcommando*. At the western side of the dyke there is a ditch draining into the River de Zoom (see aerial photograph).

Lambert, Kipp and a few other soldiers climbed up the dyke and crossed the curve of the river, using the railway line, but they immediately came under machine gun fire from the stove factory. They then spread out over the track right and left, and dashed for cover. Kipp found cover behind an iron pole, which was hit by bullets several times.

All around him men were dying. It wasn't until Lambert yelled: 'Are you coming with me, or have I got to go alone?' that the remaining men scrambled up the dyke and got over the river and the ditch.

They then ran about 30 meters over open terrain under German fire until they reached the wall of the stove factory. It was pitch dark. Kipp heard the impact of a bullet to the left of him. A voice asked: 'Are you all right?' A man answered 'I don't know yet.' A bullet had gone into one side of his steel helmet and and out the other without touching him.

They reached the brick wall of the stove factory. Two men put their hands together to make a step, which the other soldiers used to climb the wall. Two men stopped on top of the wall and hoisted the last men over. Then a count was made: of the 30 men in the company only 13 had made it into the factory.

Only when they were in the factory did Lambert tell Kipp about the change in plans. A Company was to establish a position in the factory, and after five minutes C Company was to follow them in by the same route. Then D Company was to attack from the other side across the River de Zoom into the adjacent laundry building, and clear the stove factory and the gin factory. Lambert's men only learned later why C company had failed to join them.

Unknown to them two things had gone wrong. The artillery was to have put the stove factory under shell-fire before the arrival of A company. However, they had missed their target and hit C Company position, killing and wounding many

CANADA AND NOORD-BRABANT: AN ETERNAL BOND – 17

Laundry building 'the Zoom' after the battle. Arrow: Window from which Holst has aimed at Armstrong and the Dutch Red Cross nurse.   PHOTO COURTESY: L.P. ROOSENBOOM

soldiers and putting a stop to their advance. As a result the attack by D Company had to be postponed.
But Lambert and Kipp didn't know of these events at the time. All they knew was that there were 13 Canadians in a factory full of Germans.

They waited until it was clear that nobody was coming to assist them. Lambert then decided that A Company would clear the factory on its own. Lambert ordered them to spread out and fight from many points so that the Germans would think they were facing a complete regiment. They fought among the machinery, up and down stairs without being able to see anything or anyone clearly in the pitch darkness. The only light came from the muzzle flashes of rifles, but these betrayed the position of the rifleman and he then became a target. A German launched a grenade, thus

18 – CANADA AND NOORD-BRABANT: AN ETERNAL BOND

The gin factory. Arrow: the green door through which Kipp escaped.

Under: Wall of the stove factory. Hole caused by a bazooka.

PHOTOS COURTESY: L.P. ROOSENBOOM

betraying his position. That was one adversary less. Sometimes the Canadians had the upper hand, sometimes it was the Germans. The stenguns of the Canadians weren't very useful as they had got clogged with mud during the swim across the river and the ditch.

The two sides were shouting curses at each other, and the Canadians cried 'Come in and get killed, we are the Lincoln and Welland! Come on and taste our knives.'

The Germans were also outside the building. They blasted holes in the walls with bazookas, and then threw hand grenades through the holes.

But in the end the superior Germans numbers were too much and threatened to overwhelm the Canadians. They were driven back to the wall by which they had climbed in. The Germans shouted 'Surrender!' But then a soldier came up to Kipp and said: 'Sarge, we came here to fight and not to surrender.'

After that the fighting died down. The Germans knew that the Canadians couldn't escape and they were probably just waiting for the morning light when they would be able to see their adversaries.

Then suddenly a German opened up with an MG.42 machine gun behind Kipp. Bullets were flying everywhere. The muzzle blast blinded Kipp for five minutes. He went after the man who had just fired, but he couldn't find him. Kipp climbed up a small tower, but he still couldn't see anything.

Soon after somebody came to Kipp and told him that Lambert wanted to see him. They talked over their situation and what they should do. It was appparent that they weren't likely to get reinforcements, and that they might have been written off as dead or captured.

It was at this point that Lambert asked Kipp if he could escape from the factory to let the Colonel know of their desperate situation. Kipp agreed that there was no other choice and said he would give it a try.

Kipp took off his equipment and ammunition, which he gave to his men. He only kept a .38 revolver and three rounds of ammunition. From one dark spot to another Kipp moved through the Geman lines. Later he found out that he had gone through their first aid station. He finally came into a driveway, not making a sound. The moon was up and he could see the beginning of a blue sky as dawn approached.

He slipped along the dark side of a wall till he reached a green door. He stepped through it on to a pavement and decided to go south where he could see the town. He used a big church steeple as beacon.

But he knew that there were Germans about. If they saw him sneaking down the road, they would certainly shoot him. So he decided to walk like a German officer, banging the steelcaps on his shoes loudly on the pavement, as if he owned the city.

A German saw him as he passed a sidestreet and asked for the pass-word. His first thought was to shoot, then he thought ' That may let all hell loose,'so he didn't react but just marched noisely on. Other Germans called out from their sheltered positions, but he still coolly marched on, ignoring them. Close to the laundry, he met a German who was in such utter confusion that he didn't know how to react. Kipp slipped by and jumped into the river.

He then climbed up the river bank, slowly, because otherwise the Germans could have located him by the sound of dripping water. He immediately went to ground behind one of a row of tank obstacles which had been built by the Germans.

It was only in 1986 that he found out why the Germans hadn't shot him. The day before, they had shot their own commander in the leg when he didn't react on being challenged for the pass-word he had completely forgotten, after consuming too much of the gin factory's produce. The German soldiers evidently didn't want to risk repeating their mistake.

But then there was another danger. Some Canadians had taken up position behind those tank obstacles. Kipp therefore had to make sure he was recognized as a Canadian. He sneaked behind the obstacles whispering ' Lincoln and Welland.' He immediately bumped into a bunch of rifles directed towards him, and made himself known. The D Company was there, the Company that should have attacked the factory in the last phase of the attack.

Kipp asked who their commander was and was told 'Armstrong,' whom Kipp knew well. He ordered: 'Get him over here and tell him that Kipp is here.' A few minutes later Armstrong arrived. Kipp said to him: 'Take me to the Colonel, in a hurry.' They then ran to the HQ of the D Company, jumped into Major Swayze's jeep and drove through the city to the HQ in the hotel *De Draak* on the market square.

They entered the hotel where Colonel Wotherspoon and Lieutenant-Colonel Cromb were sitting at a large table. Cromb was so astonished to see Kipp that he almost fell out of his chair.

Kipp rapidly told them what had happened.

He was then taken into another room where a Dutch nurse took care of him. This Red Cross nurse, the day before, had walked along the path behind the tank obstacles with Armstrong. After the war Kipp found out that a German had aimed at the two of them from a window of the laundry, but didn't shoot them because he respected the Red Cross Insignia.

After twenty minutes the Colonel asked Kipp to come and see him. He was told to join C Company that was already trying to enter the stove factory. When he arrived at the railway, the C Company had come under heavy machine gun fire and were retreating, carrying their dead and wounded.

So Kipp returned yet again to the Hotel de Draak, where he was told to catch up with Captain Martin who was on his way to the railway with his Brengun Platoon. When Kipp arrived, Martin had already lost several of his men. After these two fruitless attempts, Kipp decided on his own initiative to try to contact his own A Company.

He went back to the place where he had swum over the River de Zoom the night before, and found a soldier who told him that D Company had meanwhile managed to enter the stove factory. A Sherman tank of the South Alberta Regiment had taken up position close to the remnants of the dynamited bridge. The driver of the tank stood beside his vehicle. A German soldier came out of the laundry building and asked for cigarettes. The tankman threw a complete pack of cigarettes to the German, after which he went back into the laundry building. The tankman had made a temporary bridge over the stream using a door he had taken from a demolished house. Kipp crossed the river via this bridge and entered the stove factory.

He found himself in a storage room , filled with vats marked by the skull and crossbones sign, full of deadly acid. He heard a noise from behind the vats and immediately shot at them ; the impact of the bullet gave rise to a terrible noise. A German jumped from behind the vats, calling *Kameraden* (Comrades) and was followed by a dozen other Germans with their hands up. Kipp took these prisoners back across the bridge and turned them over to some other Canadians. Then he went back into the factory, to find the D Company men. He searched several rooms all alone until he saw a closed door. He felt that something was wrong, something was unusual. If D Company men had been there, they would have looked into that room and would have left that door open. It was a small detail, but it put him on his guard.

Then he noticed that the door was open, just a very small crack. He tiptoed to the door and saw a dead German lying on the floor. But then he saw the dead man open his eyes! Kipp kicked the door open and aimed his rifle at him. He ordered him to get out of the room with his hands up, which the man did. Kipp saw that he had a Luger in a holster, and Cromb had expressed his wish to have a Luger! And now Kipp could get one for him. The German was a sergeant of the Sixth *Fallschirmjaeger* (Parachute) Regiment. From the way the man looked at him, Kipp knew he was an extremely dangerous prisoner, who could jump on him at any moment. So he took no risks. He ordered the paratrooper to put the Luger on the floor and step away from it. He picked up the Luger and at that very moment a man from Battalion

Headquarters came in. That man obviously had not the slightest idea how dangerous it was in the factory, because he wasn't even carrying a weapon. Kipp made sure the man knew how to handle a Luger and then handed the German over to him, to take him across the river. Kipp also gave him strict orders to take the Luger to Lieutenant-Colonel Cromb. Later Cromb thanked Kipp for the weapon.

From this point I hand over the story to Kipp
I was still searching for D Company . I found them and said: 'Come on, don't just stand there.' I went around a brick wall and came to the same open space I had escaped through the night before. To my surprise I saw several German soldiers with a dead D Company man at their feet. I glanced back to see if the D Company men were following me, and, to my shock, saw there was a German officer behind me, aiming his rifle. Later on I heard that the German had tried to shoot me, but his gun had failed to go off, and I hadn't even noticed it . I and my gun were both facing away from him, so I simply lowered my gun and nodded to the officer to look behind him. To my amazement he actually looked around. He turned back to me, but by then I had swung around, lifted and aimed my gun. We stood there aiming at one another with only a few feet between the muzzles of our rifles.

If one of us had pulled the trigger, the reflexes provoked by the impact of the bullet would have caused the other man's rifle to fire as well. So we didn't shoot. We looked at each other, knowing that death was close for both of us. And then the officer mumbled something out of the corner of his mouth to his men, who left through the green door one after

Aerial photograph of 27-09-1944.
1: railroadditch, 2: stove factory, 3: ginfactory, 4: laundry building.
Z: the River the Zoom. >>>>>>: Escape route of Kipp.
Curved arrow: the River the Zoom curving under the railroad.
Both arrows: attack route to the stove factory. © TOPOGRAFISCHE DIENST, EMMEN

another; then the officer also went –backwards- to the door. We didn't lose sight of one another for a second; when the officer arrived at the door he raised his right hand and waved goodbye. I waved back; he then disappeared through the door. Only then did I start to breathe again.

After this episode I resumed my search for my A Company men. I entered the factory again, and then all of a sudden the door of a toolshed opened! I immediately pointed my rifle at the door, ready to fire, when Lambert came out with a few men. I said:'Lambert, you bastard.' They had been hiding in that room after they ran out of ammunition. They looked like a bunch of ghosts.

Then another man who had missed the others in the darkness came out of a little room. It was Wally Balfour, who, when he ran out of ammo, had hidden under a workbench in that room. He had a bullet in his right upper leg. In the middle of the night, two Germans had entered the room, sat on another workbench, put a candle between them, lighted it and eaten some food. Wally hadn't made a sound. After a quarter of an hour the Germans left. Wally remained under the bench until he heard us talking. Many years later in Toronto he told me that never in his life had he been so happy to see somebody as at that moment!

The A Company men and I left the factory and I counted how many of us had survived. The answer was: only 8 out of the 13 that had entered the factory. But these 13 had eliminated 27 Germans.

The 8 of us then drove away by jeep. We had fought for 17 hours.

I was exhausted, I felt sick, in short I was utterly finished. I just kept on moving like a robot. All around me, German shells were exploding. I came to the street were the English teacher lived. All the houses looked similar, but something drew me to one door. I knocked and the door was opened by the English teacher himself. It was indeed the house where we had drunk a toast only twenty-four hours before.

I went to sleep there and slept for forty hours. I had asked my Dutch hosts to awaken me after eight hours, so I could rejoin my unit. They told me that they had tried and failed to wake me and so had asked Lambert what to do. He said simply 'Let him sleep'.

That was Kipp's account.

In those forty hours that Kipp lay deeply asleep, celebrations were taking place in the city centre.

The Canadians who fought in the factory were all members of the Lincoln and Welland Regiment.

Lambert was decorated with the Military Cross for his role in the fighting.

The Canadians who were killed in the fighting are buried in the Canadian War Cemetry in Bergen op Zoom. The grave of Lambert, who was killed in January 1945 in the very bloody fight at Kapelsche Veer, is also there.

The Germans were part of the Sixth *Fallschirmjaeger* Regiment. That regiment had been under the command of *Oberstleutnant* Dr.Friedrich-August Freiherr von der Heydte up to October 25. He had been decorated by the Fuehrer with '*Das Eichenlaub zum Ritterkreuz des Eisernen Kreuzes*' (oak leaves added to the Iron Cross) on September 30. At the same time the Fuehrer had given him the task of assembling a parachute unit to be deployed in the Battle of The Bulge, which the Germans were already planning. Therefore, Von der Heydte gave up command of the Sixth *Fallschirmjaeger* Regiment just before the battle with the Canadians.

On October 26 he had presided over a meeting at which the Mayor of Bergen op Zoom was present. The result of this discussion was that after consulting with his Commander, Lieutenant-General Chill, he promised not to defend the city under the strict condition that the population didn't take any action against the retreating Germans. Von der Heydte said farewell to the Mayor with the words; '*Ich wünsche Ihnen viel Glück mit ihrer Stadt*' (I wish you all the best with your city).

The greater part of the city had therefore fallen into Canadian hands practically undamaged after heavy fighting, to the south.
 This was in sharp contrast to the heavy battles that had taken place on the northern edge of the city, where the Germans fiercely defended the *Panzersperre* de Zoom. This *Panzersperre* served as the northern section of the antitank ditch that the Germans had dug all round the town.
 The *Panzersperre* was thus meant to defend the city against an attack from the north, but in the end was used as a defence against an attack from the south by the Cana-

CANADA AND NOORD-BRABANT: AN ETERNAL BOND – 29

May 1986. Meeting of Canadian and German War Veterans on the Lincoln Memorial bridge. 4th from left: Sgt. Charles Kipp; 4th from right: Carl Heinz Holst; 3th from left: Sgt Bill Kipp, brother of Charles; 3th from right: G.le Coutre; on both flanks: German Veterans. To the left of the group: tankobstacles, behind which Kipp sought for cover.

PHOTO COURTESY: MARGARET KIPP

Brownsville, Ontario, Canada; 28-10-1999. Charles Kipp and Jan Luijten relive the toast, exactly 55 years ago to the day.

© THE TILLSONBURG INDEPENDENT NEWS.

Row of toolsheds; Lambert hid in one of these.

Under: Railroadbridge over the River the Zoom used in the attack on the stove factory.

© R. VAN DEN BERGE

dians. This explains why heavy fighting only took place along the northern edge of the city.

In May 1986 a meeting was arranged between Kipp and veterans from the Sixth *Fallschirmjaeger* Regiment by Mr. Roosenboom, who was the owner of the factory which now stands on the place of the former laundry building.

At this meeting Kipp met the German Lieutenant who had stood face to face with him in 1944: Carl Heinz Holst. They shook hands on the bridge built at the spot where Kipp had swum the River de Zoom.

Also present was Holst's commander: Le Coutre, the man who was shot in his right leg because he had forgotten the pass-word after having drunk too much at the gin factory. After the battle the bodies of two Germans had been found at the bottom of a gin vat. It is suspected that they had drunk so much gin that they fell in the vat and drowned.

After the meeting on the bridge, Kipp and Holst placed a wreath together at the Canadian War Cemetry.

The *Bundestagabgeordnete* (Member of the German Parliament) Guenter Volmer, who had taken part in the fighting as *Oberjaeger* then spoke and said: '*Wir haben euch nie gehasst.*' (We never hated you).

The title *Lost Patrol* is derived from an article in the Daily Mirror of October 30, 1944.

The subtitle *A battle of madmen in the dark* was used in October 1944 by Gordon Sinclair in his daily *CBC* radio programme about the course of the Second World War.

The Rosary Para from Germany: how Bergen op Zoom was spared

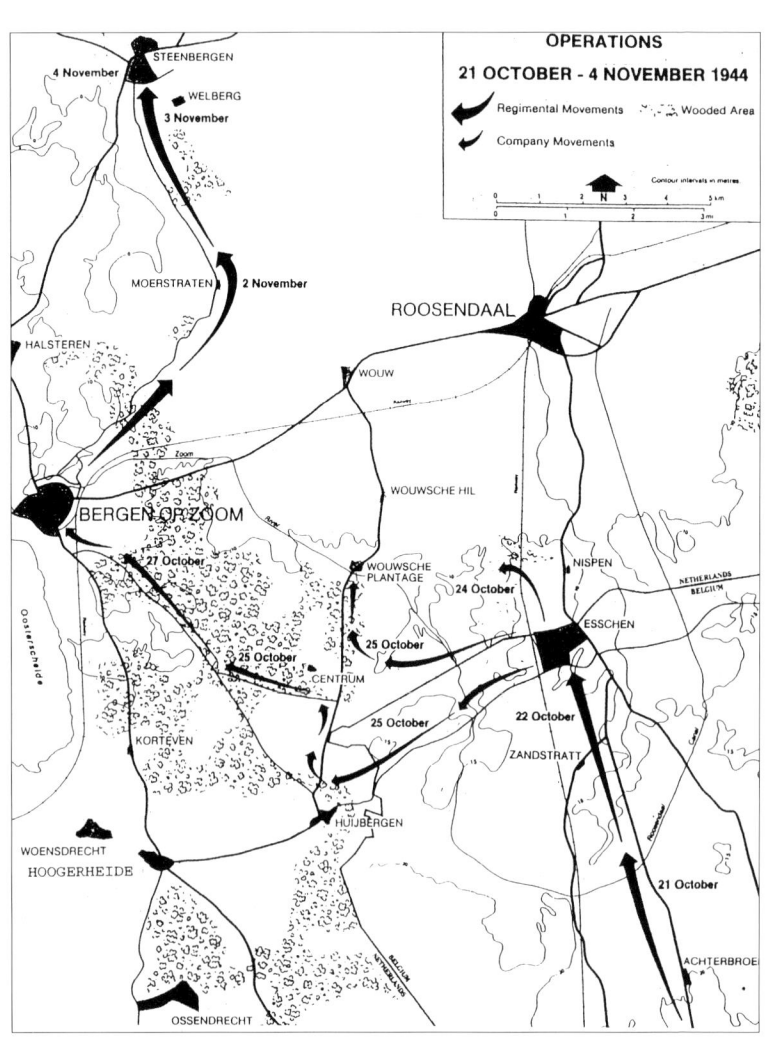

Friedrich-August Freiherr von der Heydte was born in Munich on 30-03-1907. In his younger years he was given an excellent education. As a child he had an Irish and a French governess: he therefore became fluent in English and French, languages he brushed up even more during his Gymnasium years and during his study at the Konsular-akademie in Vienna in 1927.

During the period 1925-1926 he received a military training as Cadet of the *Reichswehr*. When Hitler came to power, he quickly enlisted in the army on March 1, 1934. He therefore couldn't finish his law studies, even though he was preparing a *Habilitationsschrift*.

After the outbreak of the Second World War he fought on several frontsectors: France (Maginot line) 1940, Crete 1941, Russia (Leningrad sector) 1941, North Afrika 1942, Italy 1943, Normandy 1944. During the Italian campaign he met the Pope.

Audience of Friedrich-August Freiherr von der Heydte with Pope Pius XII

Rome, January 1943.
Von der Heydte recalls the visit.

Oberstleutnant Friedrich-August Freiherr von der Heydte, October 1944.

'Members of the German armed forces were strictly forbidden by a *Fuehrerbefehl* to attend an audience of the Holy Father. This 'greatest general of all times' did not in my opinion, however, have the right to forbid a Roman Catholic from visiting the head of the Roman Catholic Church.

On my way to the audience room I wore my dirty and worn-out Afrika uniform with my decorations: the *Ritterkreuz*, the German Cross in Gold, the two Italian silver Courage Medals. The Swiss Gards presented their halberds, the officers of the Nobelgard[1] lowered their swords as I went past.

Directly after entering the audience room I was brought by an attendant into a separate room. Three German officers in civilian dress and three other German military men were already present. The Holy Father wanted to speak with the German soldiers separately. As soon as he entered the room he started to speak with the nearest soldier, thereby solving the problem of how to greet him: we were unsure whether to stand to attention or to kneel. The Pope shook hands with all of us and asked about our families and our war experiences. He hoped that I would add the *Eichenlaub* (oakleaves) to my *Ritterkreuz,* a wish that was to be fulfilled later. Towards the end he asked about my uncle, Klaus Graf von Preising, at that time Bishop of Berlin, adding: "he was, no he still is, my best friend."

After this conversation the Holy Father lowered his red Cappa from his shoulder with inimitable grace, gave everyone a rosary and me two, one for my wife, and blessed us: at that moment it was only natural for us to kneel.'

---

1. Nobelgard: composed of members of the Roman Nobility; abolished by pope Paulus VI

The Cadets of the year 1925; 4th from left: von der Heydte, the only one who survived.

The Battle of the Scheldt, October 1944
This Battle had two distinct phases.

First phase
On October 5 the Canadian forces crossed the Dutch border at the village of Putte. The Canadian offensive that then started was aimed at the conquest of the Kreekrakdam -the Beveland isthmus, to be followed by the capture of the islands of Beveland and Walcheren. As long as these islands were still in German hands, the harbour of the already liberated city of Antwerp could not be used for the supply of the Allied Forces.

The Germans took positions on the elevated ground in and around the villages of Hoogerheide and Woensdrecht. The Sixth Parachute Regiment was brought in with all speed to strengthen the weakened German forces. This elite regiment was commanded by Oberstleutnant Friedrich-August Freiherr von der Heydte, and became part of the *Kampfgruppe* Chill.

The Canadian forces belonged to the Second Canadian Infantry Division, part of the First Canadian Army under the command of General Crerar.

The protracted battle that followed resulted in great losses, especially on the Canadian side. Fierce house-to-housefighting raged for many days in both villages, especially in the village of Woensdrecht that went on from October 7 to 24 and resulted in many casualties.

The local population suffered heavily. Many villagers were evacuated to Bergen op Zoom, where the population was hiding in cellars, as the city was hit many times by Canadian artillery.

After the heavy fighting in and around Woensdrecht the Kreekrakdam was reached by the Canadians on October 24. Beveland was conquered soon after, because, according to von der Heydte, it was defended by a bunch of '*Magenkranken*.' (Bellyachers). Von der Heydte had great respect for his adversaries; high ranking officers fought with their soldiers, even in the frontline!

In the following days the Canadians captured a few little villages on the road to Bergen op Zoom.

After the conferring of the Ritterkreuz in the Führer Headquarters on 23-06-1941.

Second phase of the battle (Operation Suitcase)
On October 18 the Fourth Canadian Armoured Division of the First Canadian Army arrived at Brasschaat in Belgium to take over the task of the exhausted and decimated Second Infantry Division.

This Fourth Division consisted of the South Alberta Regiment (SAR) and three infantry regiments. Each regiment had added to it a SAR squadron, the Lincoln and Welland Regiment received the A Squadron, the Algonquin Regiment the B Squadron, the Argyll and Sutherland Highlanders of Canada the C Squadron.

This division was at a lower than normal strength because of the casualties suffered in the heavy fighting at Moerbrugge and Moerkerke in Belgium during the liberation of the 'Breskens Pocket'.

This force advanced in Belgium to the north to the town of Essen, then made a turn to the west to cross the Dutch border on October 23 and reached the villages of Huijbergen and Wouwsche Plantage.

The fighting for the village Wouwsche Plantage took three days up to October 26; during this fight the Canadians became cornered, they could only be rescued by the launch of many flamethrowers.

Fierce tank battles then raged in the woods of Wouwsche Plantage, whereby many Sherman tanks were put out of action, especially because the area was heavily mined.

In the end the city of Bergen op Zoom came in sight and the Canadians reached the outer limits of the city via two roads.

Bergen op Zoom, October 1944

On October 26 von der Heydte summoned the burgomaster of the town, Mr. Dr. H.A.F. Lijnkamp to his HQ in the former Cantonal Court, Grote Markt 27, a stone's throw away from the Deaconal Roman Catholic Church.

He started by requiring the evacuation of the population of the city, so that the inhabitants wouldn't hamper the Germans in their defence of the city. The city was full of refugees, who had fled the heavy fighting to the south of the city. The city, that was surrounded by an anti-tank moat dug out by the Germans during the war, was destined to be defended in house-to-house fighting.

The burgomaster refused, even after the demand was repeated twice.

Mgr. dr. Ch.A.M. van Dam.

PHOTO COURTESY REGIONAAL HISTORISCH CENTRUM, BERGEN OP ZOOM.

Shortly before this the Dean of the Catholic Church, Mgr. Dr. Ch.A.M. van Dam, had begged the Germans from the pulpit of the Deaconal Church to save the city and its inhabitants. Von der Heydte, whose HQ was only a few houses away from the church, will certainly have attended the Sunday mass on October 22, in which van Dam begged to save the city. Von der Heydte's devotion was such that he always attended Sunday Mass, even during fighting.

The day before this meeting, on October 25, von der Heydte had said farewell to his forces in a *Tagesbefehl* (Routine Order) in which he mentioned that Hitler had decorated him on September 30 with the *Eichenlaub* (Oakleaves) added to the *Ritterkreuz des Eisernen Kreuzes*, that he had received on June 23 in the year 1941 after his airborne operation on the Island of Crete. The telegram in which the decoration was announced to him had reached him on October 23. The Fuehrer had given him the task of assembling a paratroopers unit destined for the Battle of the Bulge.

At this crucial moment in the life of the aristocrat von der Heydte certain things will have come to his mind. He was a devout Catholic, Goering had called him the Rosary Para. His Catholic Christian Belief was rooted in the history of the Holy Roman Empire and also in the idea of a united Christian Europe as expressed by Dr.Otto von Habsburg, to whom he later dedicated his autobiography.[2]

---

[2]. The title of his autobiography: *Muss Ich sterben, will Ich fallen* is the first line of a family song, written by one of his ancestors in the eighteenth century.

Colonel Gordon Dorward de Salaberry Wotherspoon, 'Swatty'.

By virtue of his education, honour and devotion to duty were his central guidelines. His high standard of behaviour as a German officer was taught to him by his father, Major in the Königl. Bayer.1. Schweren Reiter-Regiment.

As he had come to the conclusion that Hitler was destroying the German people and that the war the way he waged it could not be won, he had in 1942 contacted the group around Klaus Graf von Stauffenberg.

During the meeting with the burgomaster he will certainly have rememberd the audience with the Pope who had expressed his wish about the *Eichenlaub* to his *Ritterkreuz des Eisernen Kreuzes.* The reminiscense of the blessing by the Pope, combined with the request by the Dean of the Roman Catholic church might have played a crucial role when he decided, after consultation with his commander, Lieutenant-General Chill, to release the city. Von der Heydte ended the meeting by saying to the Burgomaster: '*Ich wünsche Ihnen viel Glück mit ihrer Stadt.*' (I wish you all the best with your city.)

The freeing of the city of Rome on June 4 of the year 1944, two days before the Normandy landing, was perhaps a precedent.

On October 27 the Canadians stood before the city. The Underground Forces had informed the Canadians that the town had been abandoned by the Germans. This sounded unbelievable to the ears of the commanders of the South Alberta Regiment and the Infantry Regiments. They fore-

Lieutenant-Colonel William 'Bill' Cromb.

saw heavy fighting in the city that was the last barrier for the clearing of the waterways to the city of Antwerp.

At some stage, however, they became convinced and the commander of the South Albertas, Colonel Gordon Dorward de Salaberry Wotherspoon, would have said to the commander of the Lincoln and Welland regiment, Lieutenant-Colonel William 'Bill' Cromb: 'Hell, Bill, let's take the damned place.'

The Salaberry Wotherspoon then gave Lieutenant Danny Mc Cleod the order to enter the city with his Sherman Tank. At the same time he ordered two Stuart Reconnaissance Tanks to reconnoitre the northern edge of the city. Mc Cleod was accompagnied by Ad de Munck, a member of the Dutch underground forces.

The Tank of Danny Mc Cleod was on its journey to the the centre surrounded by a cheering crowd and Danny reached the market place only after a one hour drive at four o'clock in the afternoon. The much faster Stuarts reached the northern part of the city already at a quarter past three.

The writer remembers very vividly the sound of the enormous rejoicing in the centre of the city. He – then 12 years old – immediately ran to the market place, but he didn't reach it, however, as he came under Canadian shellfire, meant for German forces to the north of the River the Zoom.

This shellfire is engraved in his memory; it was only by immediately jumping into a shelter that he survived.

Because the city , that was meant to be defended as a hedgehog position to the last ditch, was released by von der

Chicago: Greeting by US-General Maxwell Taylor, town commander of Berlin.

Heydte, many Canadian as well as German lives were certainly spared. This is also true for the inhabitants of the town.

Von der Heydte landed with a new parachute regiment in the Ardennes in December 1944. He got an insignificant arm wound in the fighting there. Although he thought himself able to keep on fighting, he nevertheless gave up and surrendered on Christmas Eve to the Americans, but sent his soldiers back in the direction of Germany.

He was a prisoner of war for three years, in the beginning in England.

Knights of the Holy Sepulchre; to the right behind von der Heydte: Prince Xavier de Bourbon.

With Gilbert Renault, "Remie", Head of the *Résistance*.

In 1948 he resumed his University Career. He became a Law Professor in Wuerzburg. He also had an advisory function in the Bundeswehr, where he became a General.

Because of his many contacts, he was also active in politics in post war Germany.

His efforts for a Christian Europe and for Christian education brought him the Papal Decoration of Comtur with the Order of Gregory with star. His efforts for a French-German reconciliation and his attitude during the war has brought him the appreciation of the French Resistance.

KAPELSCHE VEER: WHERE SEEKING AFTER PRESTIGE CAN LEAD TO

There are no bad regiments,
there are only bad officers
(Field-Marshal Lord Slim)

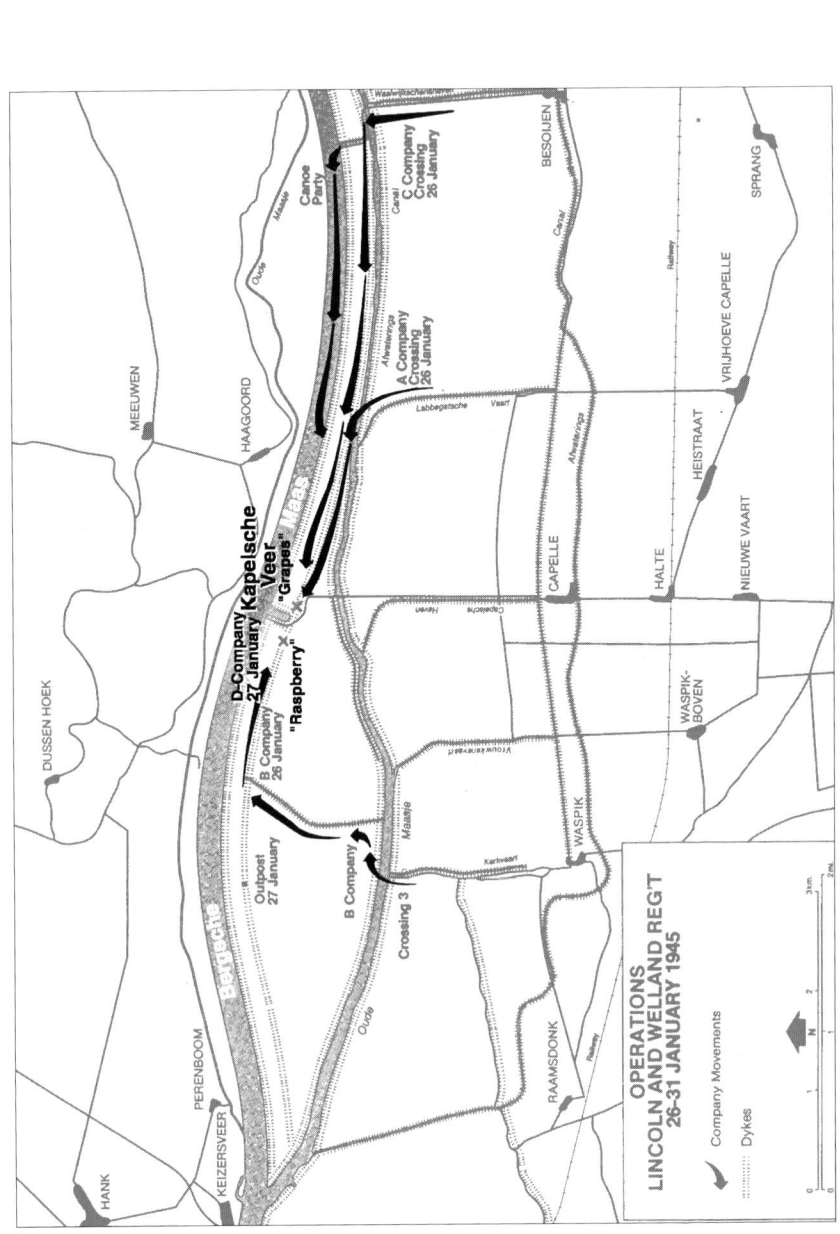

By the end of 1944 the advance of the allied forces on the western front had come to a standstill. In the province of Brabant the River the Maas had become the frontier, patrolled by German as well as Canadian soldiers. Meanwhile winter had started and it was to become one of the most vicious in human memory.

On December 16 the Germans started the 'Battle of the Bulge', in Europe known as the Ardennes Offensive. The retake of the harbour city of Antwerp was the aim of this German Offensive.

The German High Command had planned a second offensive, also targeted at Antwerp, from the still occupied northern part of the Netherlands, to start if the Ardennes Offensive had advanced far enough. The code-name of this second German attack was: *Fall Braun* (Case Brown).

In order to have a good starting-point, the Germans had retained a springboard south of the river the Maas: a small island to the north of the village Capelle, between the Rivers the Bergsche Maas and the Oude Maasje (see map).

On the northern edge of this island, on either side of the ferry bridge of the Kapelsche Ferry, stood on a dyke the only two houses of the island: the roadman's house (code-name:

Grapes) to the east and the ferryhouse (code-name Raspberry) a little further to the west.

Connected to the cellar of Grapes the Germans had excavated in the dyke a complete system of tunnels and slit-trenches. This complex constituted the Bridgehead of Kapelsche Veer. A supply line to the complex across the River the Bergsche Maas was maintained by boats.

From this fortification the Germans had an excellent field of fire on the treeless island.

The meadows of the island were laced through by many ditches. The only roads with a somewhat stable underground that could by used for an attack on the Bridgehead, were on top of a few dykes with steep slopes amidst the boggy and inundated land.

On these dykes attackers were always visible for the defending Germans.

The Allied Command was aware from Intelligence at an early stage of the Battle of the Bulge that the Germans were planning a second attack to be launched from the Bridgehead Kapelsche Veer. The Allied Command had therefore prepared a plan to eliminate the Bridgehead.

PLANNING AND PRESTIGE

No battle plan survives the first contact with the enemy, as the saying goes in the Pentagon. Seeking after prestige, however, can go on because of a failure to perceive that the original plan is outdated or useless.

The defense plan on the German side.
Army Group H, commanded by Colonel-General Student, received the task of carrying out the German plan. A unit of this Army Group, the Sixth Parachute Division commanded by Lieutenant-General Hermann Plocher, was assigned to defend the Bridgehead. This Division was composed of remnants of several diverse army units. Orginal para's were only a tiny minority. The experienced core of the Division was also charged with the task of training young green soldiers so that they could get battle experience. These last soldiers served in a rotation system.

Student was determined to defend the Bridgehead to the last ditch, even at the time when he knew that an attack on Antwerp would not take place, after the failure of the Battle of the Bulge. He hoped to draw in and mislead the allied forces.

Plocher regularly tried to convince him of the uselessness of the operation, but all in vain.

The plan of attack on the Allied side.
The First British Army Corps under the command of Lieutenant-General Sir John Crocker was positioned in the province of Brabant opposite the German Army Group H.

The Polish Armoured Division, being a part of this Army Corps, commanded by Major-General S. Maczec, got the task of eliminating the Bridgehead.

The attack, taking into account the condition of the terrain, was performed by infantry only, supported by artillery.

A first attack was made in the night of December 30/31.

This attack was a complete failure, as was a second attack in the night of January 6/7.

The German defense was too vigorous. Apart from that, the weather was very bad. The weather in the last week of December and the whole month of January was extremely cold. In freezing temperatures water surfaces became solidly frozen. Many times it was snowing and foggy. The ice was nevertheless too thin to bear the weight of the soldiers and army vehicles. The slit trenches and the foxholes that had to be dug into the frozen dykes were frequently full of icecold water so that many a soldier suffered from frostbite and had to be evacuated.

Moreover, on January 8 the Germans inundated the island by dynamiting a hole in the north dyke of the River the Oude Maasje, to the west of the demolished southern entrance bridge to the island.

After these Polish efforts an attack was launched in the night of January 13/14 by a unit of the Royal Marine Commandos. This attack also ended in failure.

These attacks were made when it was already clear that the Germans would not launch a second offensive.

At the turn of the year the Battle of the Bulge had come to a standstill. The target of Antwerp was beyond reach.

Around January 4 the Canadian Command had received information that the Germans would not launch an attack via Kapelsche Veer anymore.

However, General Crocker was afraid that after these failures the morale of his soldiers would be even more under-

Colonel-General Kurt Student.

Lieutenant-General Hermann Plocher.

Lieutenant-General Sir John Crocker.

mined, due to the widely held belief in the invincibility of the German soldier. That is why he was determined to carry out the already outdated plan.

Crocker decided, now that the Polish and British had not succeeded in eliminating the Bridgehead, that time had come to trust the task to the Fourth Canadian Armoured Division commanded by Major-General Vokes. This division consisted of the South Alberta Tank Regiment and three infantry regiments; the lion's share of the attack was for the Lincoln and Welland Infantry Regiment (*The Lincs*) that in October 1944 had been involved in heavy fighting north of Bergen op Zoom. The regiment was composed of mainly new reinforcements; only a few men who landed in Normandy were still with the regiment.

The Argyll and Sutherland Highlanders of Canada were also to participate in the fighting.

The Germans sometimes called the Canadians the British SS, because they were always successful in almost impossible fights, and because they fought in a sometimes rather ruthless way. They were not pleased, however, by this reputation.

At this time the Division was no longer under the command of their competent commanders, Colonel Gordon Dorward de Salaberry Wotherspoon and Lieutenant-Colonel William Cromb. They had been temporarily assigned to other tasks. These two commanders were appreciated by their subordinates. De Salaberry Wotherspoon was respected by his superiors and he was known for daring to refuse tasks

Major-general Christopher Vokes.

which he considered useless. This last character quality was unfortunately missing in his successor.

Operation Elephant

The attack over the dykes on the Bridgehead Kapelsche Veer was planned to start at daylight with three companies of Lincs, two approaching from the right and one from the left (see map). In order to obtain a maximum surprise effect it was decided to refrain from a preliminary artillery barrage. An extensive smokescreen was planned in order to make the attackers invisible.

As the German defenses could only be destroyed by means of flame throwers, Wasps (flamethrowers on carriers) were brought in as well as Lifebuoy Flamethrowers, to be carried by individual soldiers.

The uncompromising determination of Crocker was clearly demonstrated by the unlimited amount of material made available to Vokes. An enormous total of about 300 guns and added mortars was brought in. A colossal amount of ammunition was supplied, for example more machine-gun ammo was supplied than the amount used in the battle of El Alamein. Whatever Vokes asked for, it was supplied to him.

Vokes himself had many objections against the attack. That was why he asked for 15 canoes to be flown in from Canada. He hoped that this would take so much time that the operation would be cancelled by a new situation. Crocker, however, was so determined that this request was complied with without delay. This small gain of time, however, Vokes did not use to reconsider the risks of the attack.

This absence of introspection, combined with the lack of courage to express dissenting opinions to his superiors by Vokes, combined with the determination of Crocker, became a fatal combination of two characters. Also, neither had gained the insight that the whole operation had become outdated due to the failure of the German attack in the Battle of the Bulge.

The responsibility for the now impending catastrophe has frequently been put on Vokes; in fact, the responsibility rests with the combination of both characters.

The determination of Student as well as of Crocker was based upon a reaching of prestige by both men.

Plocher could not convince Student, and Vokes did not dare to contradict Crocker.

The only man who could have blocked Crocker was his commander, General Crerar, commander of the First Canadian Army. But he did not do that.

> *War's object is victory, not the Victoria Cross*
> (Ronald Lewin).

The attack
On January 26 at 7.15 a.m. the attack started. For the attack routes of the three different companies of the Lincs: see map. The Argyll and Sutherland Highlanders of Canada followed C Company of the Lincs.

The canoe party with 15 four-person boats started at the same time under the cover of an extensive smokescreen.

Under continuous German fire from the opposite side of the River the Bergsche Maas the sappers had constructed at the crossing point of C Company a bridge on top of the remnants of the demolished bridge over the *afwateringskanaal* . This bridge, called 'The mad whore's dream' by the soldiers, was finished just before the start of the attack.

It was the idea that the attack would be finished before noon; in the end the attack lasted five days. Within only two hours everything went wrong. The direction of the wind changed and the smokescreen offered no protection anymore, but instead caused respiratory problems in the Lincs and the soldiers manning the boats. These boat soldiers, who were meant to attack the bridgehead from the river came immediately under fire from the opposite side of the River the Bergsche Maas. Only one boat crew managed to get ashore, but it was short of the intended beachhead.

The attacking Lincs lost in a short time many of their officers, amongst them Major Lambert, the commander of A Company. He had penetrated into the outer limit of Grapes.

The Lifebuoy flame throwers did not function at all, as the soldiers who carried these heavy items only with great difficulty reached the top of the icy dykes, because the snow clogged underneath their shoes. Once on top of the dyke, they were visible and were therefore immediately shot. The Wasps slipped down from the icy dykes because of their weight. Only one Wasp succeeded in reaching Grapes and shot a flame into it: it was immediately noted and put out of action. The fighting was mainly man-to-mancombat when the Germans, emerging from their underground trenches, regularly appeared behind the Canadians.

In the night of January 26-27 the first tank crossed 'The mad whore's dream' bridge. In the following days a few Sherman and Stuart tanks crossed the bridge or reached the island by means of a raft that was used close to the crossing point of B Company. These tanks frequently bogged in the mud of the dykes. One Stuart tank, bogged on the eastern side of Grapes, resisted all attempts to move it so that the sappers were obliged to make a road diversion around it.

Gradually the Canadians reached their targets. Even if they took them, they were soon driven back again.
    The battle ended early in the morning of January 31. This was not because of the elimination of the Germans, but because they retreated over the river.

General Student was replaced by Colonel- General Johannes Blaskowitz, who ended the defense of the beach head.

The writer was able to interview two members of the Lincoln and Wellands who participated in the battle: Charles Kipp and Walter Balfour. These two also participated in the Battle of the Lost Patrol in Bergen op Zoom.
    Both men described the battle as bestial.

To give an example: at a certain moment a Linc lay on the ground with a German on top of him; at the moment the German was on the point of putting a knife in the Linc, another Linc held a gun barrel against the head of the German and blew him up.
    Wally Balfour reached Grapes directly after Lambert. A German came out of a tunnel to the left of Wally. Balfour

Major Herbert Owen Meredith Lambert, M.C.

shot the man, a handgrenade fell out of the man's hand, exploded and Wally was hit in his left arm. He kept on fighting; he stood up on the slippery slope of the dyke when another piece of shrapnel hit him in the right buttock and left his body via the right hip.

He was brought to the crossing point of A Company. There Kipp carried him on his back to a boat that brought him to the other side. Kipp then said: 'Kid, they shouldn't do that to you'

Wally was called the Kid in the regiment, because he entered the regiment at the age of 17; in January '45 he was only 19 years old.

Six soldiers were decorated after the fight; the highest decoration, the Distinguished Service Order was for the commander of B Company: Major E.J.Brady.

The losses on both sides were staggering; many hundreds, with the Canadians suffering more than the Germans.
 The Canadians who were killed found their last resting place on the Canadian War Cemetry in Groesbeek. A few of them were buried in the Canadian War Cemetry in Bergen op Zoom. There too Lambert was buried.
 Close to him are buried three Lincs whose remains were found over fifty years after the battle.
 On November 2, 2001 two of them were reburied with full military honours by present members of the Lincoln and Welland Regiment.

Literature

Doorn, J. van, J.S. Bos, *Slag om Woensdrecht: bevrijding van de Zuidwesthoek*, Stichting Historisch Onderzoek Tweede Wereldoorlog, 1995.

Graves, D.E., *South Albertas, a Canadian Regiment at War*, Robin Brass Studio, Toronto, 1998.

Hayes, G., *The Lincs: a history of the Lincoln and Welland Regiment at war.* 57-94. Alma, 1986.

Heydte, Friedrich-August Freiherr von der, *Musz ich sterben – will ich fallen*, Kurt Vowinckel-Verlag, Berg am See, 1987.

Holst, C.H., *Fallschirmjaeger-Regiment sechs: Kriegstagesbuch vom 6 september bis 5 november 1944*, von der Heydte.

Kipp, C.D., *Because we are Canadians; Memoirs of world war two.* Douglas & McIntyre, 2002, in press.

Roitero, D.L., *Fall Braun: de strijd om Kapelsche veer. 1944-1945*, H. Gianotten, Tilburg, 1995.

Rogers, R.L., *History of the Lincoln and Welland Regiment at War*, 191-209, 1989.

Wood, H.F., *Operation Elephant*, Canadian Army Journal, 8-12.

Appendix

Twee pagina's uit Daily Mirror van 30 oktober 1944.

Daily Mirror MON., OCT. 30

HEAD OFFICE:
Geraldine House, Fetter-lane, E.C.4. Holborn 4321.
And at
42–48, Hardman-street, Manchester, 3. Blackfriars 2185.

Full Moon Tomorrow.
MOONRISE—5.40 p.m.
MOONSET—7.14 a.m.
BLACK-OUT TIMES:
LONDON 6.7 p.m. to 7.21 a.m.
BIRMINGHAM 6.12 p.m. to 7.30 a.m.
BRISTOL 6.17 p.m. to 7.31 a.m.
LIVERPOOL 6.19 p.m. to 7.34 a.m.
NEWCASTLE 6.4 p.m. to 7.37 a.m.
GLASGOW 6.12 p.m. to 7.51 a.m.
PENZANCE 6.30 p.m. to 7.43 a.m.
SOUTHAMPTON 6.13 p.m. to 7.26 a.m.

13 saved by a swim

Continued from Page One

tered in little tinkling pieces, as if Jerry had thrown a vase at you. I had one burst between my boots.

"Our grenades were much better. I know that because the area around the factory was littered with dead Germans—but we didn't have nearly enough. We didn't dare waste a grenade. When it was all over we had two left.

"I ordered the men to run all over the darkened factory, yelling like hell to make Jerry think we had a regiment. We never fired two bursts from the same spot. As a matter of fact, we fired damned few bursts our

Sten guns had clogged getting across the canal. We were caught with our Stens down.

"We were calling the German paratroops every dirty, filthy thing we could think of, and maybe we laid it on a bit too thick because he came for us as if he didn't mean one of us to get away alive. Whenever we taunted him he'd fire and give away his position.

"I told the sergeant to crawl out somehow and get back to the regiment to tell them we were still alive. After he'd gone we sat around waiting for the end—we felt sure we were goners and that was that."

Then the sergeant took up the story — Sergeant Charles Kipp, of Ontario.

"Just Kept On"

"It was a clear moonlit night. After I left the factory, leaving my gun and remaining ammunition behind me, I took a bearing on the church steeple in Bergen-op-Zoom and started off down the middle of the street. I was challenged three times by Germans, but I just kept on.

"After I had swum a canal, a voice which I recognised as Canadian challenged me, and he sure sounded good. I never thought I'd live to hear another."

Sergeant Kipp reported to the brigade commander. Two efforts to reach the surrounded men. Both failed.

A major and a trooper finally managed to improvise a bridge across the canal at a point where it was only 25ft. wide, using a door broken off a nearby house and timbers hauled from the wreckage of a shelled home.

Finally a group of men led by Sergeant Kipp fought their way across.

"I saw Captain Lambert coming out of the building with the other fellows dragging after him, dead tired but grinning," said Kipp. "I thought: 'My God, they're ghosts.' I was so happy I nearly cried."

PHILIPPINE TROOPS NOW READY FOR A NEW POUNCE

AFTER striking up to the northern end of Samar Island, U.S. troops now hold positions from which they can launch an offensive against Luzon, main island in the Philippines

Alexon "SIZE RIGHT"

For your nearest stockist write to:
ALEXON & CO. LTD.
ALDERSGATE STREET, LONDON, E.C.1

12,000-POU
HITS TIRPI
HIDE-

A DIRECT hit was scored on the Tirpitz, 45,000-tons "white elephant" of the German Navy, when Lancasters attacked it with 12,000lb. bombs yesterday.

The planes made a round trip of 2,400 miles to carry out the attack, and got through despite a screen of destroyers, smoke ships and A.A. shore batteries, as well as natural allies in northern darkness and fog.

The Tirpitz was moored near the south end of Haakoy Island, four miles due west of Tromso, and had been compelled to leave her other "hide-out" in Northern Norway from the Russian advance from Finland. She was trying to escape from Kiel through Alten Fiord.

A brief wireless report sent immediately after the attack and received while the Lancasters were still flying home, said that though clouds seriously interfered with the attack, at least one direct hit was obtained on the battleship with a 12,000lb. bomb.

Yesterday's success was the second time the Tirpitz had received a direct hit with a 12,000lb. "earthquake" bomb dropped by the RAF. In September she was attacked by planes using a Russian base near Archangel.

Then, the attacking Lancasters flew 1,750 miles, the longest flight ever made by any plane carrying such a bomb load.

The raid from Russia was the seventh of a series of attacks

Bulgaria to feed Greece

The Bulgarian armistice terms announced last night closely follow the pattern of the Rumanian and Finnish terms. Also they place an obligation on Bulgaria to make amends for the wrong done to Greece and Yugoslavia.

Immediate food supplies must be delivered for the relief of the population of Western Thrace, Greek Macedonia and Eastern Yugoslavia, rendered destitute by Bulgaria.

Bulgaria is a rich agricultural country, and, according to some reports, better off for food than any country in Europe.

The armistice takes effect from last Saturday.

Vicar is "ashamed"

Continued from Page One

as a counterfeit system animated by Satan," and said he believed the reason for the fierce fighting on the European

"FRANCO WILL GO —EVEN IF IT TAKES 5 YEARS"

SENOR J. Alvarez Del Vayo, last Republican Spanish Foreign Minister, in an article which will appear in the American magazine, "The Nation," declares:

"We Spanish Republicans are determined to finish with Franco, whether we are helped or not.

"It may take six months, a year, five years, but we shall overthrow him, no matter how sympathetic Mr. Churchill may feel towards him.

"But the men and women of the United Nations, who understand that peace may be ruined by the Fascist plot now in preparation, also have the responsibility to decide whether the Fascist dictator of Spain shall or shall not be kept in power."

MUSSOLINI'S HOME TOWN SEIZED

Polish troops advancing four miles in Italy have occupied Predappio, Mussolini's birthplace, though the enemy is still holding the northern part of the town.

This advance has considerably increased the menace to Forli, now only four miles away.

what is in my mind or to according to my conscience."

Mr. Green, who is 61, and who has been the vicar of St. Nicholas's for twenty-five years, has two sons serving in the Forces.

In the current issue of his own parish magazine he refers

> Fallschirm-Jäger-Regiment 6
> — Kommandeur —
>
> Gefechtsstand, den 25.10.44
>
> ## TAGESBEFEHL.
>
> Der Führer hat mir am 30.9.1944 das Eichenlaub zum Ritterkreuz des Eisernen Kreuzes verliehen. Diese Auszeichnung gilt nicht nur mir persönlich, sondern in erster Linie dem Regiment, dessen Führer und Vertreter ich bin. Sie ist die Anerkennung der Leistungen des Regiments, vor allem Euerer Leistunge meine alten Kameraden aus der Normandie. Euerer Einsatzbereitschaft, Euerer Tapferkeit, Euerem Kampfeswillen und Euerer Härte verdanke ich die Auszeichnung mit dem Eichenlaub: Euch gilt mein Dank!
>
> Ich kann diesen Dank nur dadurch abstatten, dass ich Euch die gleiche Kameradschaft halte, die Ihr mir gegeben habt und das gleiche Vertrauen entgegenbringe, mit dem Ihr mir in harten Gefechten gefolgt seid, und dass ich in Führung und Sorge ebenso alles einsetze, wie Ihr im Kampf alles eingesetzt habt.
>
> Mein Dank gilt vor allem auch den gefallenen und verwundeten Soldaten des Regiments, die in Pflichterfüllung bis zum Letzten das höchste Opfer gebracht haben. In stolzer Trauer gedenke ich der Toten des Regiments, in treuer Verbundenheit der verwundeten Kameraden!
>
> Meine Freude über die Auszeichnung mit dem Eichenlaub wird leider wesentlich beeinträchtigt durch einen Befehl des Fallschirm-Armee-Oberkommandos, der mich von der Führung des Regiments zu anderer Verwendung abberuft. Ich brauche keinem meiner alter Kameraden zu sagen, wie schwer mir die Trennung von dem Regiment fällt, das ich aufstellen, ausbilden und in schweren und wechselvollen Kämpfen führen durfte. Die Zeit, in der ich an der Spitze des Regiments stand, gehört zu der „schönsten meines militärischen Lebens. Ich war ungeheuer stolz, Euch führen zu können, Soldaten, die pflichtbewusst und begeistert jede, auch die schwerste Aufgabe so gelöst haben, wie es von unseren Vorgesetzten erwartet worden ist, die hart und zäh in der Verteidigung ausgehalten und ungestüm und furchtlos im Angriff vorwärts gestürmt sind. Ich danke Euch allen für das was Ihr unter meiner Führung geleistet habt: Führern und Unterführern, Jägern und s. M.G.-Schützen, Meldern, Fernsprechern und Funkern, Sanitätsdienstgraden, Kraftfahrern — allen die selbstlos Ihr Letztes für dass grosse Ziel gegeben haben, und die alle mitgeholfen haben, dass der Name unseres Regiments bei den deutschen Truppen überall geachtet und beim Feind gefürchtet ist.
>
> Ich verspreche Euch, dass ich die Kameradschaft, die gemeinsames Erleben in harten Tagen des Kampfes zwischen uns gegründet hat, Euch weiter halten werde, auch wenn ich nicht mehr Euer Führer bin; ich bitte Euch, auch mir diese Kameradschaft zu bewahren.
>
> Ich bin überzeugt, dass Ihr Euerem neuen Kommandeur ebenso folgen werdet, wie mir, dass Ihr ihm das gleiche Vertrauen entgegenbringt und dass Ihr unter seiner Führung ebenso tapfer kämpft und ebenso entschlossen aushaltet, wie bisher. Auch Euer neuer Kommandeur ist ein Frontsoldat, der weiss, was der Landser braucht und wo ihm der Schuh drückt.
>
> Haltet die Fahne des Regiments hoch, reiht den stolzen Leistungen des Regiments in der Normandie und in Süd-Holland neue Taten an, die den bisherigen entsprechen; kämpft getreu der Überlieferung des Regiments und steht Eueren Mann so, dass Ihr Euch vor unseren Taten nicht zu schämen braucht; macht das Wort wahr, das ich Euch im Februar in Wahn bei der Aufstellung des Regiments zugerufen habe: „Wenn alles zusammenbricht und Welle über Welle über unserem Volk zusammen schlägt, dann wird noch ein Fallschirmjäger meines Regiments dem Schicksal trotzen und im Sturm und Ungewitter die Fahne hoch über die Fluten halten, auf der ein Wort in leuchtenden Buchstaben steht: „Grossdeutschland" — und dieses Wort „Grossdeutschland" wird er hineinrufen in das Toben des Sturmes, und stolzer sein als alle Sturmflut, die uns bedroht, soll dieser Ruf sein eines Fallschirmjägers vom 6. Regiment".
>
> gez. HEYDTE
>
> Oberstleutnant und Rgts.-Kommandeur.

Tagesbefehl.